T0149801

THE UN. ᴜBLISHED CITY

THE UNPUBLISHED CITY

Curated by Dionne Brand

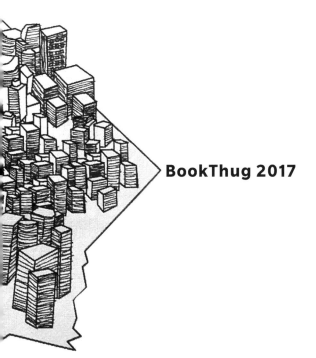

BookThug 2017

The production of this book was made possible through the generous support of the Toronto Arts Council (TAC) and the International Festival of Authors' (IFOA.org) Toronto Lit Up programme.

Toronto Lit Up, spearheaded by the TAC and IFOA is designed to spotlight Toronto's writers and empower local artists with book-launching presentations.

ISBN 9781771663731

The Unpublished City was conceived to show the (Multipli)City of writers that call Toronto home; that the City of Toronto might hear the wonderful voices of the City's own true imaginaries. The idea here is to read 'unpublished' not simply as not in print, but as the narratives, and imaginations of the City that are present, and not yet fully realized, nor acknowledged. In these stories and poems we apprehend what lies on the surface of the City's glass walls, in the depths of its rapidly and perennially urbanized landscape, and in its bristling and multilingual streets.

Dionne Brand

Contents

Ian Kamau — Wilton Street | 1984 — 9

Nadia Ragbar — Gore Street — 13

Chuqiao Yang — Thick As Thieves — 15

Twenty Years Later — 17

Rudrapriya Rathore — Canaries — 19

Sofia Mostaghimi — The Day You Were Born — 21

Katheryn Wabegijig — On This Red Path — 23

Doyali Islam — 43rd Parallel — 26

Adnan Khan — All I Can Tell You — 28

Phoebe Wang — The Invigilator — 30

Canisia Lubrin — Into Timmins — 33

David Bradford — Why Can't We Live Together — 35

If This Box Is Solid Brown — 36

Laboni Islam — First Shakespeare Class, 9/11 — 38

Terminal 3, 2002 — 40

Sanchari Sur — Mars In Scorpio — 42

Shoilee Khan — The Itch — 45

Nicole Chin — Parhelia — 48

Diana Biacora — Inang — 50

Dalton Derkson — hart house — 53

schoolboy, near-fall — 56

life after wrestling — 58

Simone Dalton — Undersigned — 60

About the Authors — 65

WILTON STREET | 1984
Ian Kamau

It's the time of day when the sun casts long grey and blue shadows on the pavement and the light filters softly through the air that drifts around in the lavender sky. It is warm, but the warmth is periodically sliced by the sharp edge of abrupt gusts of wind. The cool breeze tumbles through every open space and around every corner. There are orange and yellow leaves collecting in corners where the building meets the sidewalk, and where the sidewalk meets the street. They are held in the cropped green grass of David Crombie Park that is laid out in front of us. Fallen from the trees that are placed throughout the park the crisp leaves make a delicate scrapping sound as each gentle gust drags them across the red brick and over the grey cement. They scrape the pavement skipping and shivering as they go. It is early September.

There is a borrowed car with a door swung open over the sidewalk, colourful parking stickers in the windshield, the rear seats pushed forward all the way, the trunk exposed. The space behind the drivers seat is filled with an assortment of mostly beige coloured cardboard boxes sealed with clear plastic tape stacked from window to window floor to ceiling. My mother shifts her weight from foot to foot watching, has cut each section of tape that seal these boxes with scissors and labeled each box according to its contents. Each second-hand cardboard box, collected from the Pilipino corner store or the No Frills grocery close to the corner of King and Jameson has a dry smell, some with a slight aroma of its former contents; tropical fruit, a broken egg, spilled Coca Cola from a punctured can.

Just as my mother has cut each piece of tape with a pair of silver scissors, or ripped it with her teeth when the scissors were not immediately accessible, she has also written carefully on each box. The writing is in marker on the top flap of the individual boxes, it is sometimes red, sometimes black, and sometimes green. The bold and sweeping handwritten script reads: "living room," "bedroom," "kitchen," "Roger books, living room," "Claire books, desk," "Ian's room, toys"; my mother organizes and executes this system. There are plenty of boxes labeled "books," more than any other; their contents are predominantly my father's.

My parents, Claire Prieto and Roger McTair, both in their late thirties, stand on either side of me talking through the moving process with each other on the shallow slope of the red brick sidewalk in front of a ten-story medium-rise apartment; it is 1984.

My parents have made their first film and are in the process of working on two more. My mother a film producer, my father a writer and director: they are two of the first three black filmmakers in Canada, my mother the first and only black woman to do so thus far. She is taller than your average woman, possibly an inch shorter than my father. She is slim with a golden brown complexion and a mass of tightly curled hair pulled off of her face by a scarf that covers part of her forehead and half of the crown of her skull, letting the hair explode out of the back in every direction.

My father is slim but muscular, "sturdy" as my mother would say, with a beard that is carefully pruned which frames the dark skin on his round face. He is average height, with a short afro that he pats down to keep its shape, casually dressed with a pair of rounded and slightly oversized glasses that rarely leave his face for more than a moment. He wears a t-shirt, a pair of jeans and a simple silver bracelet that never leaves his right wrist and must be bent if it were to be removed.

My parent's volley words above my head infused with pronounced Trinidadian accents which hold a distinct Caribbean melody. My father is laid back, the move will happen as it happens; he enjoys the social aspect of the moving experience. My mother plans to get the job done as quickly and efficiently as possible, her mind is not fully at rest until she completes her chosen mission: all of the boxes in the apartment before the sun disappears below the city skyline in the west. She attempts to influence my father to focus more on the task at hand and to galvanize his friend to execute the task quickly and effectively. My father's friend moves boxes from the car to the sidewalk, from the pavement to the lobby, through the glass doors where they sit by the elevators. They exchange words and joke with each other while shuffling back and forth, speaking in sugary Trinidadian tones, laughing buoyantly and mischievously. I quietly peer around the Neighbourhood, bursts of cool air push by whispering as they go, swirling and circling gently around us. The wind sways the tiny hairs on my arm over my skin like the branches in the trees and blows through the big curls on my head.

My mother, noticing the temperature, crouches down, one knee placed lightly on the brick below, and pulls the zip on my little blue jacket upward toward my neck. The motion is quick, making a soft metallic sound like a wasp buzzing up a windowpane trying in vain to find a way out. I pull my chin to my neck for fear of the metal zipper pinching my skin; my brow tilts downward, my eyes straining to see the tab that is too close to view clearly. All I see is my mother's gentle hand, her long fingers forcing the stubborn tab upwards over my collarbone.

The air carries the smell of burnt sugar from the Redpath Sugar refinery on the lakeshore only a few short blocks away, the scent drifting through the crisp late afternoon atmosphere reminding me of the brown sugar burnt in the pan when mom starts her stewed chicken–my grandmother's recipe. Mom rises from her crouching position, resting her hand gently on one side of my upper back between my shoulders and my neck. Wilton Street, a short block in the middle of Esplanade, is laid out in front of me interrupted in the west by George Street and in the East by Frederick Street. This is one of my first memories, not only of my Neighbourhood, but also in my life. It is the weekend before my fifth birthday.

GORE STREET
Nadia Ragbar

She would have to murder him. Stella watched her neighbour from the front porch, watering his piece of the sidewalk. He saw her, and with a grunt, raised his hand. Stella glared down at the crochet spiralling furiously in her lap. He deserved everything coming to him. She'd make up a dish of blood chориço and send it over with Debbie. She imagined him unable to sleep at night, going down to the kitchen in his underclothes, eating forkfuls of it over the sink; a sickly fluorescent bulb lighting up the whole place, exposing every grotesque detail of his paunchy body and his dirty home. Her wild magic still potent, he'd be dead by the end of the week. She'd be sure to get her dish back before then.

"Mãe, it's time to come inside. I'm going to the mall—you can't sit in the sun all day. Have you seen my white sweater, Mãe? Where the hell did I put it?"

Debbie held the screen door open with one socked foot as she wheeled Stella back inside.

"Do you wanna eat lunch now, or wait till I get back? Sammy! Get your shoes on, we're leaving soon! Ok, why don't you eat now, Mãe? I already made a sandwich."

Stella didn't know why Debbie pretended she had a choice about anything. She was sitting with her chair wheeled up as close to the table as possible, one hand, a hawkish claw, shielding the side of her face. Debbie handed her mother a plastic cup of water with her pills. Stella had to take three gulps to carry the huge things down. Water dribbled down the corner of her mouth.

Sammy came running into the kitchen with one shoe on and his arms outstretched, hugging Debbie around the knees, "Mamma! Can we go to park after?"

Debbie was looking down at him, laughing: he had on Stella's enormous prescription sunglasses.

He tore back out of the kitchen, bumping into the wheelchair: "Sorry Vovó!"

Stella wanted to give him a proper lashing to teach him some respect. She took a bite of her egg salad and pushed the plate away. She needed more water.

Debbie went down into the basement with a handful of towels. Mail dropped in through the slot.

"Sammy. Bring the mail to me."

Stella had been waiting to hear from her sister in Portugal. She was sure the mailman had lost or damaged the letter. For weeks she had been telling Debbie they needed to get a Doberman. She and the dog could sit on the porch and wait for the mail. That mailman would have to look her dead in the eyes as he handed all of it over, her eyes steady on him, one hand gripping the dog's collar, keeping the growling beast temporarily at bay.

Sammy ran back into the kitchen relieving his fists of matchbox cars and stickers, "Vovó! I brought you some toys so you won't be bored while me and Mamma go to the mall."

"Mail."

Sammy ran to the door and back, tossing a handful of flyers at the table, before dashing away.

Jealousy seared through Stella because she couldn't just flail and scream and run and run. She pushed the junk mail and toys onto the floor and banged her glass on the table again and again conjuring an old memory of brutal, howling winds that could uproot trees and whip the seas into delicious bloody frenzy. She didn't listen to what Debbie was yelling up from the basement above the roar and the banging and Sammy's childish laughter.

THICK AS THIEVES
Chuqiao Yang

a trio of women dry out their hangovers
at the yoga studio, lululemon instructor
with tinker bell's lost voice in the air, she
is the healthiest human they've ever seen,
contorting muscle into ball, while anne
presses her face against the rented, rancid
smelling mat in child's pose, smother me
she mumbles as vera swallows a burp

why did we eat so much garbage last night
       because you inhaled six martinis and lost a boyfriend
           does the instructor even have bones
              this is carnage, I need coffee
                  yes   yes   yes

they namaste and dip, the world outside raining
as vera removes a fake eyelash from her hair
as laura shakes her flax and chia magic juice
as anne says get that bougie stuff away from me
as they slew and halt at a coffee shop, see hot
men reading highbrow lit, intelligent
jawlines against fendi, tweed, etc.,

it smells like expresso
it smells like marriage
it smells like still drunk

a handsome dad brings in a screaming kid, one word
says anne: condoms. why is everyone here beautiful
and thin? they order their coffees, no space anywhere

they stand in the rain outside drinking coffee,
they tally up the number of times they were
strong independent women, the number of times
they ruined themselves this past year,

can we get a seat yet?
    I see a space, but it's so small
        we can squeeze in
            go   go   go

they are a trio of football players, tossing
dolled up girls in the air, stunning
the handsome hipster husbands, but success:
butts planted in a tight row on a concrete slab
drinking coffees next to the garbage can
their victory is short-lived, joykill anne says:

      eighty percent of this room
      are people on first dates
      everyone is so polite and nervous
      man that kid has a bad attitude, even
      crappier teeth, let's get some food,

so still husbandless they leave, a trio of hungover,
slick cats laughing, living, taco hunting
post-afternoon stretch, wind airing out martini
coated mouths, arms linked like paper clips,
no folly, no stranger, no linebacker able-bodied
enough to cut through this trio, these rain pruned
friends in their city of wicked deeds, rock steady,
these foul-mouthed, lippy fiends, raw-boned
hearts full of new year's resolutions,
three little gods post saturday bender,
three little queens thicker than thieves.

TWENTY YEARS LATER
Chuqiao Yang

All fathers are their daughters' dragons and dragon-slayers.

The mines in Japan are even more cautious now,
nuclear energy is ebb and flow and hazard,
we are going to Port Hope tomorrow and I
have been sweating like a pig, rent costs
a fortune these days all those years ago
we'd rationed a bottle of Coke for a week,
God we were so poor then, I'll spend my whole
life making it up to you, do you want me to
buy you a house? Had we stayed in Beijing,
maybe we'd be millionaires by now, let me
buy your friends dinner, when you were a baby
I took you down Yonge Street, you wanted to be
Peter Mansbridge but I don't think I'd live to see
you get that old, we didn't get the VISA, we
had to go to Buffalo, that customs officer
was such a cow, you were telling us you
like the song on the radio, when are you
going to find a job, I love you so much
that if I could, I would keep you safe
in my mouth for the rest of my life,
in case the world melted you,
do you think I embarrassed you in front
of your friends? I wanted to save face,
make you proud, I told them about
Hiroshima, about nuclear energy
about Port Hope, I told them about
the bottle of Coke, do you think I
said too much? I always want to

make you proud, I know that
sometimes you are embarrassed,
I know that sometimes you are
ashamed, I promise I'll spend
the rest of my life making
this all up to you.

CANARIES
Rudrapriya Rathore

A morning in winter, 2002. I am ten years old and getting ready for school. The phone rings, and from the static I know that it is a far-away call, a back-home call, an important call. *Where's mummy?* She is in the shower. I am told to find her, to have her call back. While she dials, while she waits, while she claps her hand over her mouth, I stand on the doormat with my coat on, backpack zipped and ready. We are supposed to walk down College Street to Dewson Public School.

We don't go. Instead, a few days later, we get on a plane to Udaipur.

*

Grief is a heatstroke stumble through a coalmine. Find me with my parents, thirty years deep. History has gone slower here. The cheese comes in a tin. The bougainvilleas burn like fires. The glass of milk I am given grows a skin of fat.

Everyone calls my mother *Baby*. Later, I will watch *Dirty Dancing* and never not think of these things together. My mother's mother sits on a straw mat in the middle of her home, which is crawling with relatives. A circle of women rock and pray and talk around her. Their heads are covered, eyes downturned, but the children have memorized the patterns on their saris, which is how they clamber into the correct lap. My grandmother, newly widowed, wears pure white. When she hugs me, I don't recognize her earlobes. Stripped of jewelry, they're fleshy and naked.

*

The next time it happens, we are canaries in a blackout, eating ice cream on the porch. Toronto has no power. The July sun dims to unveil a canvas of stars. Mom is on her way home from work.

The phone rings, its battery almost dead. My father says nothing during the call but he leaves me on the porch when it ends.

I find him upstairs, sobbing on the bed. I am no longer the child. The sheets glow blue. That week, I dream of a mouse in a cardboard coffin. I have to bend its whiskers to fit them in.

Again, we walk silently through airports. Smiling feels like blasphemy. In the city of Indore, the professional mourners call me *chhori*. They have black hair to their knees and they sing like they themselves are dying, whipping their heads. Or: they sing like a flock of pigeons taking flight. Like the rasp of paper tearing.

When I first met you, my father's mother says, *it hadn't rained for weeks and weeks*. I look at a second set of naked earlobes, and at her starched white sari. What a fire, I hear her think. What a fire we have been through.

THE DAY YOU WERE BORN
Sofia Mostaghimi

The day you were born there was a snowstorm. It was a few days after your grandfather's funeral. When I got to the hospital, they shoved me into a wheelchair and rolled me to a different one through an underground tunnel. Then you were just born. You plopped out like you'd done this before. That's what the nurse said. She was surprised when I told her you were my first baby even though she shouldn't have been. I was nineteen. She should have been surprised I wasn't in school. I should have been in school, not at the hospital.

I didn't want you at first. My plan was always to put you up for adoption. My plan was always to let you go. But you got there and I knew no one in this world was going to love you like I did. That's what your boyfriends might say to you when you're a little older and you're breaking up with them. Remember that's only true of your mother, maybe, and if you're lucky, of your father, too.

So I brought you home to your grandfather's house in a neighborhood called The Beaches. My step-mom wasn't home. After the funeral, she left with her newfound inheritance to see family in New Brunswick. The house was empty. It's called The Beaches, plural, but really it's just one long beach.

I was delirious from the loneliness. You wouldn't stop crying. I took you inside my coat. The wind had mostly lifted but it still snowed and by the water, a breeze still shook off of it. I considered leaving you at the shore, or resting you on top of the water, like a message in a bottle. Don't think it's because I didn't love you. Although it's true that a certain kind of love always leads to violence. I would have killed myself too. It would have been the both of us drowning in the frigid Lake Ontario, wrapped in algae. What made me decide not to? I tried. I unzipped my jacket and pulled you away from me. You weren't dressed for the weather and you had a scrunched up face. Everything hurt for you. Breathing. Feeling the air against your skin. You looked straight at me as I held you up and I thought you saw right through me even though I know that isn't possible. Babies can't see until later, until their eyes adjust. But you could. Or you did. You saw me and I was cold inside my coat where you'd left me and I crouched with you trembling near the water. I touched the water – we were the only two people on the beach – and when I touched the water, I plunged my whole arm in. The water seeped into the lining of my clothes, inside my pores. I moved you back into my jacket.

We walked back to your grandfather's house. I packed my things. I fed you by the window, because in another life where I was stable, this was our routine. I called a cab afterwards to Union Station, and because I was curious about the experience, and I didn't know when I'd get the chance again, I used the rest of my money to buy us a train ticket. We sat on the train and I watched the cars on the highway rush past us through the trees.

ON THIS RED PATH
Katheryn Wabegijig

Her head is swimming. As she reads through writings from her time spent at art school, she feels the intensity of the teachings learned. She sees the tiled files on her computer screen and delves back into the words that had once occupied and consumed her mind. These assignments, these artworks, these readings, that exposed parts of herself that needed to be seen. Parts that she herself needed to see. She feels a pull to return to this and continue her learning but a fear overwhelms as she thinks of change.

Change, though, is the foundation of her life. Back and forth, from being near to him and then to her family. One year is all she can seem to stand in one place. The loneliness, longing, anxiety and depression sets in.

Her husband is in prison. For the last 8 years she has been waiting, really, the last 24. Waiting for their chance to be together again. Truly together.

To cope, she changes. Changes her surroundings, her address, her job, her circumstance so that she may begin again. She distracts herself with change. She finds comfort and solace in newness until it is no longer new. And then, again, she cycles through.

An idea comes to her this time. A published piece of her writings and art. An account of her journey, her path. A journey of fear, catharsis, resilience, de-colonization and re-indigenization. From institution to institution. Pieces of her that she needs to share so that she may fully process her true path. To know herself.

Through everything, she has continually felt a sense of gratitude to be able to do any of this at all. While her husband sits in his cell and is able to work on his art *maybe* once a week she has had inspiring and safe spaces to create. She is grateful.

Could this be the change that she is seeking? The next step from this place of waiting that she has named "limbo"? The next step on this Red Road?

It is difficult to stay on the Red Road. The Red Path. The Good Life. An Anishinaabe way of living that she vowed to her husband and to herself that she would walk.

"I will walk with you on this Red Path as your friend, family, lover and wife.
You are my soulmate, the love of my life. I am yours throughout time.
You have my soul, heart, body and mind. Forever and always I am yours."
Those were her vows.

They married in their sacred traditional way but inside Kingston Penitentiary, within a sectioned off area, the Native grounds, inside of a teepee, surrounded by chain link fence, imprisoned by institutional walls in mid February on a cold, brisk day. They wrote their vows on birch bark scrolls. They married with their hands bound together by sweetgrass braids. He gave her a copy of *The Red Road* so that she would always remember her way. If not for him and this path she had chosen, she would not have found the motivation, the need, the courage to take these many steps. She takes these for both of them, to know herself so that she may find the strength to walk on.

Strength from resilience.
Resilience from change.
Change from loneliness, longing, anxiety, and depression.
Change from resilience.
Resilience from Strength.

The next step awaits and then, again, she will cycle through to something new until she waits no more.

43RD PARALLEL
Doyali Islam
for sertaj and Sandra

this city, a paradox
of plasma and gloves

to know a name, to never see a face

she waits and counts how fast cells settle
she notes what is bioconcave, what is sickled

amid hum and clap and unspun din
squash and push, microscopic
vision: her head bends to her work

what is more intimate than this communion?   breath hovering over
blood and spicules, fluids peritoneal and synovial
(collected aspirations of a city)

she finishes her shift, leaves behind
a white lab coat's certainty and the unknowable
pleural griefs, erythrocytic angers

the 11, the 34, the 20 to kennedy
busloads
of skin hunger

bustle and jostle, a seat, the weight of a stranger's
head nestled on her shoulder: an accident

of fatigue and proximity

to see a face, to never know a name
a paradox, this city

2   capezio, toronto – 1988

she is a poet, so
of course she sells shoes

by which i mean she spends her time

trailing and convincing wealthy customers
not to buy, and dusting while thinking of rimbaud

on break, she reapplies
her mac lipstick (a sultry red wine)
drafts an ad on scrap receipt paper

                                        wanted:
                              young & economically virile
                                patron of the poetic arts

she pays *now magazine* 45 dollars
for a print in the classifieds
(no one responds to her call)

solace in drinks at bemelmans
eggs benedict
past midnight

deep-green satin blouse, black mini, and smokey
eye attract subwayloads

of truncated desire

she sells shoes and is a poet, too
familiar with desire

ALL I CAN TELL YOU
Adnan Khan

Her parents' house is long and narrow, two windows up top, two windows on the main floor, and a tiny crack of chimney on the right side. A kid's drawing. A poof of smoke. Their lawn is brown-green and cut badly, short near the roadside, but a tuft near the windows. One car drive with a black Camry that I squeeze past. The side window over the kitchen seems like a good entry point: the motion detector light near the door comes on. I wait. My breath in the air and I'm sure there's a raccoon somewhere I can't see. No shadows, no movements. I move again.

I watched a few YouTube videos on lock picking. I don't want to break the window or cut the mesh: I want to be a ghost, to visit Becky like she is. I've been to this house only once before and that small memory tumbles at me. It was a birthday party when we were 19, and she introduced me to her parents as her friend. We had emailed before about this—I was warned—but a sling of pain came at me at that party anyway. Her parents allowed us to drink beer in the basement (white parents were always down for beer, not hard liquor) and I drank five bottles. She drank nine and vomited. I held her hair over the toilet until Bernie came down and asked me to leave. Her hair was matted to her skull skin by all that hot sweat that appears when your body moves with sickness. I held onto her nape and even then I wanted to kiss it. Her father would have seen this desire. I didn't want to hide it. I wanted that revenge, for him to wonder if we were something. I was angry at him even though she was the one that kept me hidden.

*

I can't sneak into this house without a trace. I am not a ghost. I am not a ghost. I promise I am not a ghost. In front of the Camry is a long basement window. It is thin and stretches half the length of the basement. I use my knife to cut a small opening in the mesh and pull it out. The metal against my skin in the cold. I wish there was something I could do about my skin that there was a prayer I could say to turn it into metal and gold and strong. My heart pumps for me. It doesn't matter. I'm in.

*

She moved back all her books and belongings. In our apartment she would look at me from underneath the bed sheets, her bottom half covered, her diary in her hand. She would ask me not to look at her diary. I never have—I remember once she left it on the bed and I stared at it for five minutes. It had a black cardstock cover. I opened it and read the inscription, her full name, the year, how much of a reward she would give if it was returned—20 bucks. I closed it and let it lie on the bed. Her diaries would be here in a closet. I wonder if they might be with the parents. Would they read through them? I wanted to ask her parents to let me move in to her room and let them take care of me.

A small Vans shoebox on the desk that I know is full of mementos from our relationship. It's black, small, frayed. A note might be in there.

THE INVIGILATOR
Phoebe Wang

The first to assault the invisible bastion of silence inside the centre was Felix. He shouldered through the glass sliding doors, his breath like a forge bellows, his coat and scarf and exam papers and booklets flapping in his arms like cryptic flags. Lily gladly surrendered her morning solitude to him. For an hour she'd been readying the centre, checking the roster of confirmed students, and using up her meager supply of small-talk with the other test centre coordinators.

She'd been aware, the way the inhabitants of a city under siege are aware of a gathering, faceless army, of the skid and scuffle of motorized vehicles and lumbering winter boots in the hard vinyl corridor. Her co-workers had armed themselves with cheerful greetings before unlocking the door 15 minutes before their usual time. She glimpsed their faces like frenetic masks through the glass, engulfed by students in bright parkas and defiantly pom-pommed hats they'd be forced to removed before being allowed to enter.

Felix was well known to her. He waved at her, showering pencils and crib sheets. He was a third-year student in nursing, and had a disorder known as ASUD, or Attention Surplus Underactivity Disorder. Felix squinted at her face, his eyes scanning her the dry skin on her cheeks and the oily shine of her lip-balmed mouth. He could preoccupy himself for minutes at a door handle or the tip of his pen, hence his special accommodation– six hours to write an exam when others had to write it in two.

Lily hastily seated him in the centre of a spiral of cubicles, blocked from any view of a window or door, and told him in slow low tones of his time limitations. There was already a huddle of students by the door slipping out of puffy jackets like bright caterpillars from pupas. Only one remained encased in a black ski-mask with a tinted visor, black bodysuit and skin-tight gloves. It was Hsin-yi, who had a light-sensitive condition and only took classes in the winter months. It was rumoured certain students—likely from tropical countries—murmured 'vampire' when she passed in the hallways. Though her skin didn't burn in artificial light, Lily shook her head at the thoughtless of the Prof who'd scheduled Hsin-yi's exam for this time of the day. But there was no time for suppositions. She seated her in a special 'blackout' area—amazing that the college had found room in its budget for the track curtains! Most likely the cost would have offset by the liability of future lawsuits, thought Lily caustically.

Then stuttered in several students, who, judging by their finger-tapping and distracted air, had permanent earworms. The lockers were all full now, with bags and coats dumped along the walls and assistants bumping into walls and partitions with harassed 'sorrys.' Lily looked at them like a general who did not expect her troops to survive the battle.

"Me for this hold you can please?" whispered the next student, struggling with a tangle of earphones, gloves and jacket. Just what I need now, a Syntactical Dyslexic, thought Lily, then felt thankful none of the temp staff had happened to intercept this student. She'd been trained for this.

"Sure," she paused. "Me follow."

"signs any near seated be not rather I'd," murmured the student. It took Lily a moment to rearrange this. Her head was full of a dull buzzing and her ankles were sore from the constant pacing.

"Problem no," she mouthed back. She wondered idly what his major was—Business management? Gender studies? She peered down at his test paper, and at the backwards text, experienced the dizzy feeling of looking in a fun-house mirror.

The threat of chaos and outburst, after several hours, no

longer lurked in the hallway. Now it floated in the warm air above the bent heads and around the circulating invigilators. Lily could feel it in the gaps between her fingers and her teeth. She thought of herself as a sponge, soaking up their anxiety through her performance of efficiency, though she had to admit most of them barely noticed her soft tread behind their tensed backs. Here they were gathered to write tests on material that had cost them so much to learn, and that would or would not help them in their eventual occupations. Lily almost envied their specialness, their impairments, disorders and fixations that exempted them from the ordinary masses. If she'd had the choice, which of—but this was no way to think, if she wanted to emerge from today with all her faculties intact.

INTO TIMMINS
Canisia Lubrin

Before I started working the mines we lived in Timmins, Ontario. The whole street was lined with brick houses, except the first one. It was a small shack on a wide cul-de-sac at the end of Malahat Boulevard. On the left was Whites Lane in the heart of the bush. The middle of swamps and black flies.And on the right, our neighbour, Holinger. Mr. Holinger, a giant-looking man in a top hat and tuxedo jacket, had altogether forgotten about his old life in El Paso. Here in Timmins he was, like my father, a mine prospector. The rest of Malahat Boulevard was farmers and Indians.

We had the smallest mine and to keep it going, my mother found workers at the local scotch club who knew more about grapes and bread than mining. They was mostly recent ex-pats from Italy and North Minnesota.

What of Cletus and his wife Rubina. He looked like a paramedic in his striped pants, and worked at the soap house processing animal fats. She stayed indoors as she was immobile. She still had strong, square features with her dark long hair and black nacreous eyes. At night, she filled notebooks with poems about George Washington Carver and peanuts. That day she fell into the new well that the Wajapitiskas were building and broke her spine, I was playing moggle in the field and heard her calling out: *In the name of Washington Carver, Jesus George, drown me.*

They said to hell with Timmins and moved to Iowa.

And there was Mario and Antonella Primicci. They were brought over by the Missionaries of the Immaculate Heart in their early teens. He was lean with a fat moustache and smoked a pound of tobacco daily. In Italy, his folks made life out of flour before they died of the measles. Here, he and his sister opened a bakery below the local orphanage owned by the missionaries and made all the bread we ate all year. I'd see them on the street corner with wicker baskets piled high with bread. Every Saturday after hours kneading dough by hand they'd set up cross-tables and sell. The first customer would have to be a woman. Men are bad luck they said. We all would laugh and say bad luck bad luck.

My father knew the American who traded in steel and dynamites and owned the northern railroad. When I was fifteen—and we had moved from Malahat Boulevard to Notre Dame Street—when my father needed more workers than he could find, I decided to help my father with the mine. I left school altogether and woke up at dawn every morning. One morning in October, my father was reading the paper as he usually did and found the New York Times, 1909 had wrote up on Timmins and the mines, calling us the gold rush capital of the great north. They better send us some worksmen, my father had said, I don't know who got the bright idea to free all the niggers.

WHY CAN'T WE LIVE TOGETHER
David Bradford

Here's how white a street can be lit A cozy close
circuit And still look like a fuckboy everywhere.

Even garage doors are all up in it like HIGHER
D2F CHILL and I'm like closing my eyes

for a minute Consent Not To Be A Single Being
I know I keep telling myself but then there's

danger in streetcars and the sadness in jays fans
and drake ALL OURS I mean CITY PRIDE I mean

at least two future cop choppers now low concussive
spotlights in shit bucket clouds A magic bullet sky

hard-selling the obstacle of downtown Why
more than one? The Church Fans Of The System

sounds like dumb panic but really this is
panicking The shadows off grace real good hiding

but just for a while The ash bark gone full spread
with ice water eyes Black squirrels sparkling

like warm steak knives for my twix bars This is our
City Within A Park's whole dog bowl grove marked

with an X. So bright with a good plan for death.
Wheezy stardust sucking on gold cellophane

where they buried the garrison in a gravel pit.
And we are all friends till the snacks run out.

IF THIS BOX IS SOLID BROWN
IS THAT SOUND STILL A PERSON
David Bradford

Again   palms up
blue with blood and specie
   No   I'm repeat it
        He says
                I don't
care about your
fucking change you
didn't pay for your

slice   you
    An [bates breath]

          -word not there
like an   -word-
whistle

The pecorino ATM
the cook watched over
too poor   a witness

[...]   Like an grana sausage bell

    Like tight cut-offs
buffala chamois
fontina acetate
tortoise   shit
still
too middle brackish to
play off this [hands up

and down their penny-bun skin] still
grainy as whole wheat

                                My [sighs]
first fucking time
in here and you
give me this shit

[...]   Maybe you
shouldn't come
in here   then

        Exactly what he said

Which sat so fine [sucks teeth]
with the roommate's lentils parmesan

I almost apologize for telling him

    I almost apologized for telling him

FIRST SHAKESPEARE CLASS, 9/11
Laboni Islam

I stare at the syllabus, while the professor
calls names alphabetically.   A —

We will study comedies, histories, tragedies.   B —

Today was Tragedy.
Smoke and flame. A million girders
collapsing inside and outside bodies.   C —

Not any form of faith my father taught me,
quietly upon carpet,
the ninety-nine names of God.   D —

We will learn to scan lines for stressed beats,
where breath falls, long and heavy.   E —

In *Romeo & Juliet*
I, too, will ask: *What's in a name?*
and consider the predicament of roses.   F —

Years ago, from backyard roses
emerged a bee. It stung and —   G —

a red welt bloomed,
but I have no perennial fear
of roses.   H —

I love my name, yet,
My name, dear saint, is hateful to myself,
Because it is an enemy to thee.   ISLAM —

Every face a startled mirror
where I see my self
distorted.   ISLAM — ?

What tongue shall smooth thy name?

TERMINAL 3, 2002
Laboni Islam

I have emptied
my keys & coins into the plastic bin,
sent knapsack rolling
into the x-ray machine,
walked through the metal detectors
like a stand of maples.
No sound. Random
is the word they use
to describe the way I've been chosen.
I remember a teacher
who called on students
when they hadn't raised their hands.
I knew the turning
point in the third act, could explain
light & darkness recurring
as motifs. Still,
I made myself small in my seat,
avoided her eyes.
The woman who will search me
is wearing a hijab. This is to say: *Look!*
We employ Muslims. Or,
We were expecting you.

I understand fear,
the way it plants flags,
forms an empire in muscle & marrow.
She will lead me to a private room
for the pat-down. I
will raise both hands
for the safety of this country.

If I could open my compartments, tip
my metal into the plastic bin,
they would see
that when I find a spider
in a web in a corner
that I call mine, I let it live. It lets me
live.

                  —January 29, 2017

MARS IN SCORPIO
By Sanchari Sur

1

I had neglected to remember him by the time I moved to Canada. He was my baba's friend's son. We lived at the two respective neighbouring ends that made up the tip of the boot snug between the Red Sea and the Persian Gulf.

Our fathers, who were school friends, had recently connected over email. There were talks of family visits, but nothing came of it. It was during this time that for some reason, our fathers decided that we could also become friends; in their minds, our age was an assumed bridge.

We were fourteen, that awkward vulnerable period when it was, I suppose, easier to strike up a faceless conversation.

We exchanged a few emails, talking mainly about books and movies; my Nancy Drews competing with his Hardy Boys; my love for horror over his sci-fi. We discovered that even though our afternoons had similar arcs – napping mothers—we spent them differently. While I chose to curl up with a book, his poison was trying to conquer a Roman settlement on his computer screen.

And as enthusiastic as he had been in his extensive, meditated responses, just as suddenly, he very enthusiastically stopped writing.

My Mars is in Scorpio, which is perhaps why I was quick to take offence. I never followed up, never cared to inquire why. I imagined in the new age of internet revolution when online dating was commonplace through ICQ, he had found someone in his zip code to keep him busy.

It was only when we moved to Mississauga four years later, that baba brought up his name.

"Do you remember Ronnie?" he said.

"Who?"

"Dipankar uncle's son. The one you wrote emails to."

"The one who lived in Muscat?"

"The same."

"He stopped writing, I remember."

"Yes. He died."

I had seen only one dead person in my short lifetime. She was my friend's grandmother, a stern woman laid out on the family bed, austere in her widow's sari. I was six then. I gaped curiously at her nostrils stuffed with cotton wool. It was later when I read that on dying people start leaking from places, I wondered if she had been stuffed elsewhere as well.

"Muscle dystrophy when he was fourteen," baba said, as if it was self-explanatory, "his family is in Mississauga now."

2

Muscular dystrophy is a genetic disorder that gradually weakens the body's muscles. It is caused by incorrect or missing genetic information that prevents the body from making the proteins needed to build and maintain healthy muscles.

A child who is diagnosed with muscle dystrophy gradually loses the ability to do things like walk, sit upright, breathe easily, and move the arms and hands. This increasing weakness can lead to other health problems.

There is no cure for muscle dystrophy.

3

Our families met often, making road trips, both short and long. I vaguely tolerated their daughter, Rani, a girl much younger in age, and her inane cravings for MacDonald's on these trips.

We never talked of Ronnie, but he was always there; the silent ghost hanging out with us in the living room, on the beach at Wasaga, breathing out into the January cold in New York, making a face when Rani whined for junk food, or just staring through the windows when our cars passed each other.

I hated these outings as much as I had hated Ronnie's silence all those years ago.

4

His family moved to Mumbai before the summer of our second year. They had tried, they said, but in the end, it was the cold that drove them out.

THE ITCH
Shoilee Khan

One day, while looking out at the city she had lived in all her life, the old woman felt an itch prickle up her back. It was the kind of itch that churned like exposed sprockets, the teeth murmuring against fine strands of muscles, tremors rippling through the body. The old woman tried every contraption: a long handled khunti from the kitchen, a hairbrush with copper covered bristles, even a dried palm frond she scraped across her skin while she bathed hunched on the floor of the ghusl-khana, hot water dripping off her elbows. But, the itch was persistent. Her nights were spent writhing against doorframes, her blouse unbuttoned and hiked over her shoulders in sweat-soaked folds at her neck. On the fourth day, she stood on the verandah and stared at the scum-lined pond, furious. If there were fish in that water, their bellies were bloated, their bodies warped with luminescent scales. The pond bobbed in violent greens at the foot of her building, women from the bosti smacking wet saris on its banks. The late afternoon heat rippled the water's fetid stench up, up, up over her face and the itch hummed. That's when the woman made a decision: She would climb to the roof that evening and drop from the ledge into the thick waters face first, the sludge engulfing her by the shoulders, cocooning her body, quieting this inconsolable thing.

At that very moment, the lace-hawker lumbered up the roadway, his voice cracking into the still air. Under his arm, he carried a glass-covered box fitted with spools of ribbon and lace, and over his shoulder hung a hefty bindle of useful things: yo-yos and earrings, nail clippers and hair-clips, pencils and bottles of red nail polish, the details that punctuated the lives spinning on and on in these rising cement blocks. The old woman called out to the lace-hawker and jerked down the steps, coins in hand. He unknotted the bindle and spread it out on the road. He opened his glass case.

The old woman purchased a red, plastic back-scratcher that had prongs shaped like curved fingers. Right there on the rutted roadway, she slid the plastic wand down the back of her blouse and scratched. There was a satisfying rasp. Strips of skin curled up over the neckline of the woman's blouse. She scratched again and the flesh came up thick, its underside jelly-red and gleaming. The lace-hawker gathered up the corners of his bindle and wound the sheet into a knot.

The old woman moaned, her chin to the sky. The sound was long and low and guttural and it heaved from her body in a gust. She scratched and long white strands of sinew sprayed into the dusty air. She crouched low, almost on her knees. The tenants in the surrounding flats pressed their faces against the iron bars of their balconies while the lace-hawker circled, his bindle bumping against his hipbone. The old woman's skin lay in coils at her feet and the muscles clung ragged against bone, but the itch murmured on. She flung her arms back and dug the claw of the wand into the base of her spine. She drew it up the ridge of her back, her mouth in a withered O, her pupils tiny pin pricks in the midday light. The muscles fell in meaty chunks to the ground, still pulsing. A few men wanted to reach out to grasp her wrist, or hook her by the elbow, but they balled their hands into fists, their knuckles burning.

In a few moments, there was bone. The wand click-clicked over the knobs of vertebrae, the tiny plastic fingers scraping hard and clean. The old woman sighed and sighed again. She sighed into the soft dirt, her body curving to the ground. The sound of her sighs reached the tops of all the buildings and the people standing on their balconies sighed with her, the air frothing into fog. The lace-hawker drifted into the mist of the city, and like an arc of strange fish bones rising from silt at the bottom of the sea, the old woman's bones carved into the fizzing light. At first, the surface of bone looked like a muddle of iridescent colour at play, but it was the shadow cast by the fog that gave the old woman's spine the mistaken hue. In time, the fog rose up, up, up, and the old woman's bones blared: they were gold - bright, hard, intemerate gold.

PARHELIA
Nicole Chin

What I remember most about my grandfather was the way he held a jackrabbit, gripping its neck with his thumb and forefinger and nothing else. He stood with his back to me and the blood dripped a long trail that made me think of my mother wringing out the wash, the trail of water that would follow her as she made her way from the basin to the back of the house. The edges of his sleeves were soaked like hers. His were red, hers were clear.

I stood in my parka with my hands at my sides. The sky was grey and pelting out hard bullets of snow. My face peppered pink. I had lost my mittens. My hands were wrapped in my grandfather's scarf, his own gloves much too large to stay on my hands so I was bound with cloth, my fingers peeking from the edges. I used the heel of my boot to make cracks in the ice, snapping and splintering. I bent down and put the pieces in my mouth and wrapped my tongue against them until the edges melted away. My grandfather watched me and said nothing.

We walked home. We had a sled but no dogs. What was left lay behind us; the night before, the bear who had killed one dog and left the others running. It was my grandfather who found the pack leader in the morning. I had watched from the window of the house we had stayed in overnight, the one that was not ours and that we had found, and saw him pull off his glove to touch it. He moved his hand towards the dog. It lay with its belly open, dusted with the cold. My grandfather's fingers blushed red.

My grandfather weaved my hand into his and made me walk at his pace, the rabbit slamming against his jacket. Its eyes looked at me and I watched as snow collected around the eyeball, gathering around its lashes. When I ate that rabbit, it was all I could think about it.

My grandfather brought the one dog with us. There was something about it that I didn't understand, something that made my grandfather stop. He gave me the rabbit and then bent down to grip the dog's legs. We dragged it behind us. I didn't know why. I began to believe that we were bringing the dog with us to eat. I began to wonder about those stories about saving pelts or using the bodies of the dead to keep you warm. We wouldn't be able to fit inside this small body. We needed more space. We walked home and when we got back, my mother was crying. My grandfather stood in the snow, his hands still around the dog, its hardened body against his legs. Her hands were the warmest things I had felt in a long time.

INANG
Diana Biacora

"We have to go," my mother said as she hung up the phone. "Inang is sick."

The next thing I knew, we were packed and ready to board a plane. My mother and I flew halfway across the world just to say goodbye.

When my mother and I arrived, Inang was already in a coma. All the old women in the barrio prayed around her, reciting the Rosary and offering Novenas. Her body laid on a brown wicker bed, in a room on the main floor next to the kitchen. My grandfather had it built for her some years ago when her arthritis got bad.

The evening she passed she called out the names of people who no longer walked the earth. Like Miguel, my late uncle who was bit by some bug on a Boy Scout trip and never quite made it years before I was born.

My mother placed a broken, cream colored rosary on Inang's hands when she passed. Tears rolled down her face. We said our goodbyes. The old ladies wailed.

An hour later, two stumpy women in slippers came in with a basin of water and some cloth.

Everyone was asked to leave the room. I watched, from a distance as they washed her body.

My grandfather stood by the kitchen doorway, smoking. I was

told to go out and play.

When the adults were busy planning what kind of food to buy for the lamay, I snuck back in and peeked into her room. The old ladies were gone.

She was gone; her floral dress neatly laid on her bed.

In the living room, the couch against the window had been moved, replaced by a mahogany casket in between a basket of yellow flowers on a stand and two large floor lamps. Two strange men stood over the open casket. They laughed and chatted away as their hands moved up and down her body like a surgeon's. The smell of old, expired nail polish remover left me nauseous.

For the entire week visitors came and paid their respects. The lamay was like a twenty-four hour open house. Tita Luz said there was an old superstition to never leave the dead alone at their wake. Someone always had to be awake and present, watching over them and the donation box. I spent most of my time with my cousins in my uncle's house.

"Did you know that if you see a white butterfly fluttering around right after someone's death it means their soul has gone to heaven?" my cousin Kaitlyn said. "It's like they're telling you they're okay. They made it to where they're supposed to be."

Everyone nodded. I followed.

"Or how you're supposed to cover all the mirrors in the house," Justin, my other cousin added. "Why?" I asked.

"So that you don't see something you want to see."

We all looked at each other and laughed in an uncomfortable way.

Another superstition was that visitors were not allowed to leave unfed. My mother, her brothers and sisters served puto, kutsinta and orange juice in tetra packs during the lamay. Guests gathered around the casket, chatting the night away. All the old ladies told stories of Inang and caught up on the town's gossip while their husbands smoked and played mah-jong outside the house.

When the seven nights passed there was a procession from the house all the way to the church and the cemetery. Her body rolled away in a hearse as we followed behind on foot. It was the parading of a dead body throughout town. Everyone watched from their windows, stepping outside of their homes as we passed. All the women in my family hid their faces under umbrellas while the men hid behind their sunglasses. A marching band followed behind us.

It smelled like sampaguita that day.

hart house
Dalton Derkson

i

i was the pasture.
    deer bed in the
belly of pheasant
pregnant fields
that chose to stampede east
      tward the television
    glory of a 6 footed, deep
    city.
gimme them concrete guts,
    baybay: the cigarette butts
    nd the shitbirds.
i'd gorilla'd myself a self.
      all wound
up in the act of
person,
i took the contract nd
    spit my blood to
    sign it.
i know the rules, yes:
      i fake everything
      but my own
      death.

ii

knockout
knight of
kensington.
go ahead nd trace my steps
round a stadium stretching no
further east
than spadina,   no wider
west than whatever the ones past
the park are.
this   is   my
hole nd i bathe
in its dirt.
the welcome mat is broken but the
door still works   s'well as the
other
token-terrific, city-specific shit.
i take the streetcar to a gathering of
gorillas, nd burn their wicker dicks like
candles,
all ends ablaze
in the eye of their typewriter
fire.
we'll circle the line
some 20-odd times nd make it
hard not to realize that the
seating here,
in only others' heat,
makes the one real solution
obvious:
tonite, we'll break
our bones in botch.

54

iii

how to be suspended   from a
        body that gives no rope,   has
no
                        governing
head? by being stapled to the
ceiling
with half a banana in my mouth
            reciting the alphabet aloud
while the whispering wonder
        of every other poetry captivates
in calmness.   my shoulder skin
        sores from the neighbourhood of giants
        riding atop it.   i'm in the
stadium tonite, yes, but not scheduled to
appear.
                        sorry,
but no one wants to be
        anything until they think
        they are
nd can then understand their
        trumpeting shoulda stayed
                        lily low
in something like native grass.
        something like bird
        baths.
            something like a simple
                nd untelevised stampede.

schoolboy, near-fall
Dalton Derkson

i
backwards nd dirty
like the grid road racism
of the boys at yr small town dancebar.
ugly nd useless,
not unlike having a low-lit dancefloor
in said bar that plays shania twain
nd 'fishin in the dark'
on a nightly basis.
tho, i suppose it is true
that there are limited tunes
in every superstar's repertoire
nd some are just bound
to come around more often
because they sit
on the tip
of the brain's muscly tongue.
nd while capable, yes,
of competing at higher levels —
bending knees nd swinging elbows —
sometimes machinery
just feels more comfortable
parked within the standard.
among the quancet quatro-beat
nd the typical wail
of a fiddler who sings not thru the throat
but thru horsehair
nd precision angles.
such touchy wrists nd forearms …

have you ever seen someone
grab another someone
by the crotch to the whitebread twang
of an alan jackson jukebox?
        i have.
nd i continue to see it,
almost relish in it
for the sake of being able to halo-hold
my heart above my head, shouting
        i will never be like this

                (again).

        i will never 2-step
with the girl 3 farms over who i used to
meet on the darmody grid with 4 beers
        nd 2 pairs
                of young, wet genitals
because it feels good
        to feel good about someone
                        who isn't yrself.
whose defining trait is having traded up
for what must be real bars, real dancefloors,
grown-up cocktails
                nd sidecars
built to be too small for any 2 people
to ever even t r y to fuck in:
                a stipulation learned
only thru the sweaty art of repeated, partial failure.
        like when you think you know
better than you knew better before
you never knew better.

life after wrestling
Dalton Derkson

                    a
according to the n me, this district's supposed
                                    s
to entertain me but the moneymaker in
                        g   o
the south of the city et me sh ok like
            d   i
insecure du es at a hanlan's po nt beach
                        s
party. too many people ee me. nd not
      m
just   e but that me i'm supposed to be.
                        y
the me that hasn't et slouched the dream.
                            w
the kinda me that'd make you anna name
            i   t   n
ferry term nals af er me or condomi ium
          e   s
side stre ts. omething often took nd
                    s
overlooked. there i no stage bigger than
                            he
the city. no audience hars r than its blind
                        i
mind of human mass. f i'm left alone
            s
with all the e people much longer we'll
                            b
degenerate like rotator cuffs. e sidelined by

                                                r
the fact that we'll only know each othe

              o
as what we've d ne with one another.

                k
played parts. kic ed teeth out of spotlights

            e   n
in search of fir . if this is happe ing in

                i
the present, i'm b lled from absence, tipping

                          n
scales at seven foot, two seve ty-five

              h
pounds. my shoot eight is six feet deep

      a   l   f
nd em ciated from shove ling cement or change.

                as god is my witness,
                  he is broken in half.

UNDERSIGNED
Simone Dalton

Sa'nia had a problem and a new love. She was attending to a mid-week ritual in one of her favourite haunts, a café at Adelaide and John with Italian soul and staff who remembered how she liked her Americano. As she stirred the fourth sachet of brown sugar into the steaming brew, she thought about the warmth of D's thighs against her cheek, the smells of shea butter and sweet almond oil that radiated from between them. She also remembered feeling her mother's presence in the dimly lit bedroom. A heaviness hung in the sandalwood-heavy air. "You should pray about it," Sa'nia's free therapist at the women's clinic said. Once a nun, the therapist apparently thought her God of all things also knew a thing or two about lesbian sex. And, even though the "it" on Sa'nia's mind had much more to do with reconciling the newness of this expression of her sexuality than her orgasm, she had tried last night. To pray, to ask God to bless her hands and mouth as they found and lost parts of D's cinnamon-coloured skin among the sheets. To help her enjoy their love. As the last oh, fuck, caught at the back of D's throat, Sa'nia came to terms with the bigger issue that was lurking in the dark corners of her bedroom. She hadn't told her mother about D.

A notepad sat next to her half-filled coffee mug. She had decided to write a letter to her mother. It would be a draft really, since her actual words would be transmitted by email. Save for the date, though, October 20, 2008, the page was empty. She thought about starting the letter with the tale of how she met D in the summer. She had caught a glimpse of her across the subway platform at Castle Frank station. D looked at ease in a white, men's shirt over cut-off jeans and runners. Her hair was pulled back in a low ponytail, so that her freckled cheeks were unobstructed and large eyes were the stars of her face. Back home, they would have called her a red girl. D, who discovered that she was the subject of Sa'nia's curiosity, nodded, smiled and changed platforms. By the time the train pulled into the station, D had introduced herself and left with Sa'nia's number in her phone.

She thought about telling her mother about their day-long first date. After brunch, they spent an afternoon filled with timorous looks, "ums" and "ahs" along the docks at Polson Pier. "Your fuchsia nail polish caught me off guard though," she told D, as she looked down at her manicured feet in brown leather sandals. "I'm a girl and I don't even wear pink."

"So am I."

"I know, but—you know what I mean," Sa'nia fumbled to explain her comment, kissing her teeth in the process.

Sa'nia spent the rest of the day wiping crumbs from D's lips after shared cheese pies and loukoumades in Greektown. Lips that she kissed that night outside her father's Riverdale walk-up. And Mum, I counted to ten, the way you taught me to do at three years old when I was scared. I counted to ten before kissing her. When she looked down at her page, those words were not there, just the date and scratches of blue pen ink.

Diana Biacora is a first year MFA student in the University of Guelph's Creative Writing program. She writes fiction and non-fiction. She lives and writes in Toronto.

David Bradford is an MFA candidate at the University of Guelph and leads the Slo-Po group reading series. His work has appeared in a variety of places, including *Lemon Hound* and *Prairie Fire*, and his latest chapbook, *Call Out* (Knife|Fork|Book), is forthcoming in 2017.

Nicole Chin is the author of the House of Anansi Press Digital Short, "Shooting the Bitch", which received the McIllquham Foundation Prize for best original short story. Her work has appeared in *Joyland Magazine, Room Magazine, The Puritan, Found Press* and others. She has been long-listed for the House of Anansi Broken Social Scene Short Story Contest and was the recipient of the Helen Richards Campbell Memorial Award.

Simone Dalton is grappling with the chaos of her relatively new 'wokeness' as a writer She is learning how to bring this reality forth on the page as a student in the University of Guelph's Creative Writing MFA program. Simone was born and raised in Trinidad and Tobago.

Dalton Derkson is a poet from parts of the Canadian Prairies unknown. More work can be found in *BafterC, In/Words*, and the *Toronto Star*.

Doyali Islam is the winner of *Arc Poetry Magazine*'s 2016 Poem of the Year Contest, and other poems have been published in *Kenyon Review Online* and *The Fiddlehead*. The poem " – 43rd parallel – " comes from her manuscript, *heft and sing*.

Laboni Islam's poetry has appeared in echolocation, *FreeFall, (parenthetical), spiral orb*, and *wildness*. She teaches at the Art Gallery of Ontario and Aga Khan Museum, animating the gap between art and young audiences.

Ian Kamau is a writer, music maker and designer; an artist who believes in the pursuit of actualization, especially by marginalized individuals and groups. He is interested in exploring the value of art to society. Born and raised in the Esplanade, a neighbourhood in downtown Toronto, to Trinidadian parents who immigrated to Canada in the 1970s. His parents are documentary filmmakers, his mother a producer, his father a writer and director. He grew up around ideas, social movements, education and all forms of creativity.

Adnan Khan has written for *VICE, The Globe and Mail, Hazlitt*, and others. He was awarded the RBC Taylor Prize for Emerging Writer in 2016 and has been nominated for a National Magazine Award.

Shoilee Khan's fiction has appeared in a diverse collection of magazines and journals, including *Adbusters, Room Magazine, The New Quarterly*, and *Other Voices*. She teaches English in the School of Communication and Literary Studies at Sheridan College and is the host and curator of Bluegate Reading Collective, a reading series in the Peel region.

Canisia Lubrin serves on the editorial board of the *Humber Literary Review* and on the advisory board of the Ontario Book Publishers Organization. She completed an MFA in fiction at Guelph-Humber and is the author of the poetry collection, *Voodoo Hypothesis*, forthcoming this fall from Wolsak & Wynn.

Sofia Mostaghimi's stories have appeared in *The Hart House Review, Joyland Magazine, Flyway: The Journal of Writing and Environment, Echolocation*, as well as two anthologies: *Aestas 2014: A Fabula Press Anthology* (3rd place winner) and *You Care Too Much: Creative Women on the Question of Self-Care*. A graduate of the University of Toronto's Creative Writing Master's program, she teaches, lives, and writes in Toronto.

Nadia Ragbar's work has appeared in *Broken Pencil, Echolocation, Dragnet Magazine*, and *The Glass Coin*. She lives in Toronto.

Rudrapriya Rathore's work has appeared in *The Hart House Review, The Puritan, The Walrus, Minola Review,* and *Carousel,* among other publications. Her fiction recently won an honourable mention in *Joyland'*s inaugural Open Border contest. She lives and writes in Toronto.

Sanchari Sur is a feminist/anti-racist/sex-positive/genderqueer Canadian who was born in Calcutta, India. A doctoral student of Canlit at Wilfrid Laurier University and a curator of Balderdash Reading Series, her work has been published in *Jaggery, The Feminist Wire,* and *Matrix.*

Katheryn Wabegijig is a 37 year old Ojibway/Odawa multi-disciplinary artist, custom picture framer and emerging writer who grew up in the small mining town of Elliot Lake, Ontario with ancestry in Wikwemikong, Atikameksheng Anishnawbek and belonging to Garden River First Nation. She graduated in 2016 with a BFA from OCAD University majoring in Drawing and Painting and minoring in Indigenous Visual Culture where she furthered her cultural education and continued on her path towards Decolonization through cathartic personal explorations.

Phoebe Wang Phoebe Wang was born in Ottawa and currently lives in Toronto, where she writes and teaches. She holds a BA in English from York University and a MA in Creative Writing from the University of Toronto. She is the author of two chapbooks, *Occasional Emergencies* and *Hanging Exhibits*, and was the 2015 winner of the Prism International Poetry Contest. *Admission Requirements* is her debut collection of poetry.

Chuqiao Yang's writing has appeared in *Contemporary Verse 2, Arc, Rice Paper, PRISM International, the Puritan, Room, Filling Station, Grain*, and on CBC. In 2011, Chuqiao was the recipient of two Western Magazine Awards. She was a 2015 finalist for the RBC Bronwen Wallace Award for Emerging Writers. Chuqiao was also featured in *30 under 30: an anthology of Canadian millennial poets* (In/Words Press, 2017).

Colophon

Manufactured as the first edition of *The Unpublished City* by BookThug with assistance from the Toronto Arts Council (TAC) and the International Festival of Authors (IFOA.org).

Shop online at bookthug.ca

Cover design by Emily Jung (IFOA)
Text by Jay Millar